Little Pebble™

Our Families

Mothers
Are Part of a Family

by Lucia Raatma

CAPSTONE PRESS
a capstone imprint

Little Pebble is published by Capstone Press,
1710 Roe Crest Drive, North Mankato, Minnesota 56003
www.mycapstone.com

**Library of Congress Cataloging-in-Publication Data is available
on the Library of Congress website**

ISBN: 978-1-5157-7465-5 (library binding)
ISBN: 978-1-5157-7473-0 (paperback)
written by Lucia Raatma

Editorial Credits

Christianne Jones, editor; Juliette Peters, designer;
Wanda Winch, media researcher; Laura Manthe, production specialist

Photo Credits

Capstone Studio: Karon Dubke, 5, 7, 9, 13, 15, 19, 21; Shutterstock: Angelina Babii,
paper texture, Dubova, 17, Monkey Business Images, cover, Photographee.eu, 11, Syda
Productions, 1, Teguh Mujiono, tree design

Printed and bound in China.
010428F17

Table of Contents

Mothers

A mother has children.

She is a parent.

Some mothers are called mom. Some are called mama.

What Mothers Do

Cam plays piano.

His mom helps.

9

Rayan's mom works in an office. She is busy.

Luca's mom builds houses.

She works hard.

Thomas and his mom bake. They love cookies!

Bria's moms like to be outside. Bria does too.

Anna feels sick. Her mom gives her medicine.

Mothers snuggle.

Mothers kiss.

Mothers love.

Glossary

bake—to cook in an oven

mama—another name for mom

medicine—a pill or treatment for healing an illness

office—a place where people go to work

parent—a mother or father

snuggle—to hold close

Read More

Harris, Robie H. *Who's in My Family?* All bout Our Families. Somerville, MA: Candlewick, 2012.

Lewis, Clare. *Familes Around the World.* Mankato, MN: Heinemann-Raintree, 2015.

Simon, Norma. *All Kinds of Families.* Park Ridge, IL: Albert Whitman & Company, 2016.

Internet Sites

FactHound offers a safe, fun way to find Internet sites related to this book. All of the sites on FactHound have been researched by our staff.

Here's all you do:
Visit *www.facthound.com*
Type in this code: 9781515774655

Check out projects, games and lots more at
www.capstonekids.com

Index